OPTIMISING SCHOOL LEARNING LANDSCAPES

DR DHEERAJ MEHROTRA

Made with ♥ on the Notion Press Platform
www.notionpress.com

Contents

Preface

Recently, there has been a growing focus on ***optimizing school learning landscapes****. As educators, we recognize the importance of providing students with a supportive and stimulating environment that fosters their learning and development. However, creating such an environment is complex and requires a thoughtful and strategic approach. This book provides a comprehensive guide for educators and administrators on optimising school learning landscapes. We recognize that there is no one-size-fits-all approach to creating a thriving learning environment. Instead, this book presents a range of strategies and best practices that schools can adapt to meet their specific needs and goals.*

The book Optimising School Learning Landscapes draws on education experts' latest research and insights to explore critical topics such as classroom design, curriculum development, student engagement, and teacher professional development. We aim to provide practical and actionable advice that schools can use to optimize their learning landscapes and help students thrive.

We also recognize the challenges and obstacles that schools may face in implementing these strategies and provide guidance on overcoming them. We hope this book will be a valuable resource for schools looking to create an exciting and engaging learning environment for their students.

Finally, we want to acknowledge the hard work and dedication of educators and administrators who strive to create optimal learning environments for their students daily. We hope this book will provide you with the tools and inspiration you need to continue your important work and make a meaningful difference in the lives of your students.

Author

www.authordheerajmehrotra.com

ONE

Digital Preparedness For Schools

As the use of technology in the classroom continues to grow, so does the significance of ensuring that schools are well-equipped to deal with it. As a result of the pervasive nature of technology in today's world, it is of the utmost importance for educational institutions to be well-equipped to deal with any digital emergencies that may arise, to protect their students from harm, and to provide them with the most beneficial educational experience possible.

Establishing a network infrastructure that is dependable and secure is the first step in having a digital readiness plan in place. Networks at educational institutions need to be reliable and robust to manage the significant traffic that comes with the increased number of users and devices. This necessitates routine maintenance and updating software to guarantee that the network is safe and does not include any vulnerabilities that hackers may exploit. In addition, schools should prepare contingency plans if there is a problem or disturbance with the network. This will ensure that teaching and learning can continue as normal.

Cybersecurity is an additional essential component of digital readiness for educational institutions. Since they keep vast quantities of sensitive data, such as student records, financial information, and other secret data, schools are potential targets for cyber assaults. For this reason, it is very necessary to have effective cybersecurity processes in place to defend themselves from cyber-attacks. This involves conducting routine security audits, providing instruction to staff and students on recognising and avoiding becoming victims of cyber assaults, and using anti-virus software and firewalls to guard against malware and other forms of cyber attack.

The capacity to provide possibilities for learning at a distance is one of the primary advantages of using technology in educational settings. The COVID-19 pandemic brought to light the significance of distance learning. Educational institutions must be ready to provide this alternative if crises or other situations prohibit students from receiving in-person instruction. This entails having the appropriate technological infrastructure in place, including devices, software, and platforms that allow remote learning and the requisite training and support for instructors and students to utilize these technologies appropriately.

To be fully prepared for the digital age, it is necessary to address the digital divide, which is the disparity between various demographics regarding their access to technology and the internet. The fact that many students do not have access to the gadgets or internet connection they need to engage in online learning may have a detrimental effect on the quality of education they receive. It is the responsibility of schools to strive toward bridging this difference by providing devices and internet access to students who have a demonstrated need for it, in addition to addressing other obstacles to digital access, such as cost and digital literacy.

Data management is an additional essential component of being digitally prepared. Many pieces of information, such as student records, data from standardized tests, and financial details, are compiled and stored by educational institutions. Hence, it is necessary to have adequate data management policies in place to guarantee that data is accurate, safe, and accessible to those needing it. This necessitates the establishment of guidelines and protocols for collecting, storing, and disseminating data, as well as training staff members in the ethical and responsible management of data.

Technology integration into classroom instruction and student instruction is the last component of digital readiness in educational institutions. By giving students access to a plethora of digital materials and tools, technology can increase student involvement and the quality of learning that occurs as a result. Yet, for technology to be successful in the classroom, it must be incorporated into teaching and learning in a manner that complements the curriculum and improves educational outcomes. This necessitates providing teachers with training and assistance to make effective use of technology in the classroom, as well as the use of tools and platforms congruent with the educational curriculum and the learning goals.

In conclusion, schools need to be digitally equipped to provide kids with an educational experience that is secure, efficient, and engaging. It necessitates an all-encompassing strategy that considers network infrastructure, cybersecurity, remote learning, the digital divide, data management, and the use of technology in educational practices. Schools can harness technology to give their kids the most outstanding possible education while assuring their safety and security in the digital world if the appropriate rules, procedures, and infrastructure is in place.

TWO

Classroom Management Strategies

Numerous teaching strategies can be used in the classroom to engage students, promote learning, and enhance student outcomes. Here are 100 classroom teaching strategies:

- *Lecture*
- *Demonstration*
- *Discussion*
- *Role-playing*
- *Peer teaching*
- *Inquiry-based learning*
- *Project-based learning*
- *Collaborative learning*
- *Debate*

- *Problem-based learning*
- *Games and simulations*
- *Case studies*
- *Storytelling*
- *Brainstorming*
- *Debate*
- *Questioning techniques*
- *Self-paced learning*
- *Jigsaw method*
- *Think-pair-share*
- *Graphic organizers*

- *Group work*
- *Cooperative learning*
- *Reading aloud*
- *Socratic seminar*
- *Multimedia presentations*
- *Flipped classroom*
- *Direct instruction*
- *Experiential learning*
- *Mind mapping*
- *Hands-on activities*
- *Writing assignments*

- *Reflection activities*
- *Audio-visual aids*
- *Concept mapping*
- *Visual aids*
- *Collaborative writing*
- *Think-alouds*
- *Exit tickets*
- *Peer review*
- *Reciprocal teaching*
- *Note-taking*
- *Summarizing*

- *Text annotation*
- *Inquiry circles*
- *Goal setting*
- *Debate*
- *Service learning*
- *Webquests*
- *Concept attainment*
- *Model building*
- *Differentiated instruction*
- *Scaffolding*
- *Rubrics*

- *Project management*
- *Data analysis*
- *Mindful breathing*
- *Think-pair-discuss*
- *Guided reading*
- *Learning centers*
- *Debate*
- *Classroom discussion*
- *Podcasting*
- *Research projects*
- *Poster presentations*

- *Data visualization*
- *Notebooking*
- *Infographics*
- *Video projects*
- *Peer tutoring*
- *Debate*
- *Gaming*
- *Text-to-speech software*
- *Music integration*
- *Flipped mastery*
- *Debate*

- *360-degree videos*
- *Virtual reality*
- *Augmented reality*
- *Edtech tools*
- *Social media integration*
- *Mindful meditation*
- *Gamification*
- *Personalized learning*
- *Blended learning*
- *Individualized instruction*
- *Mastery learning*

- *Competency-based education*
- *Self-directed learning*
- *Peer feedback*
- *Student-led conferences*
- *Graphic novels*
- *Comic strips*
- *Infotainment*
- *Word walls*
- *Interactive whiteboards*
- *Student choice*
- *Brain breaks*

- *Active learning*
- *Debates*
- *Direct instruction.*

These teaching strategies can be used individually or in combination to create a dynamic and engaging learning environment for students of all ages and abilities.

THREE

MODEL LESSON PLANS

Here are just a few examples of imaginative lesson plans that may be used to teach subjects like English and mathematics. Teachers can inspire students to build a passion for learning and a better grasp the topics being taught if they include creative and hands-on activities in classroom activities.

Students might find studying English and mathematics more exciting and fun with the assistance of creatively crafted lesson plans. Here are some suggestions for unique lesson plans for teaching English and Maths:

Lesson Plan in English: "Make Your Dictionary" (Create Your Own)

Students will be responsible for compiling their dictionaries as part of this lesson plan. Students can contribute new terms they discover when reading or writing, including language unique to their passions. Following this lesson plan, students may be inspired to cultivate an interest in acquiring new vocabulary and increasing their existing word pool.

Lesson Plan for Mathematics's "Mathematical Art"

The students will use mathematical ideas to create art in this lesson plan. Students may, for instance, employ geometric forms to create designs or patterns or apply algebraic equations to produce fractal art. Both of these activities are viable options. The students will be able to appreciate better the creativity and beauty found in mathematics, and they will be encouraged to explore mathematical topics in ways that go beyond just calculating equations.

Lesson Plan in English for the Topic "Alternative Endings"

In this lesson plan, the students write different conclusions about a tale they have already read. This may motivate pupils to think imaginatively and generate their ideas. Also, it may assist pupils in comprehending the components of a narrative, such as a storyline, the characters, and the conflict.

Lesson Plan for Mathematics Titled "Maths in Real Life"

Students will apply mathematical ideas to situations that they encounter in their everyday lives with this lesson plan. For example, students may determine their classroom size or utilize ratios to modify recipes. Students will be able to enhance their ability to solve problems and see the practical applications of mathematics with the aid of this lesson plan.

English: "Collaborative Storytelling" Lesson Plan

This lesson plan includes having students work in groups to construct a tale. Every student contributes to the narrative, in turn expanding on the concepts presented by their classmates as they go. Students that do this may improve their creative writing abilities and their ability to collaborate and communicate with their peers.

Lesson Plan for Mathematics' "Math Olympics"

Students will compete in a Mathematics Olympics event if they follow this lesson plan's instructions. Students have the opportunity to compete against one another in a variety of math-related activities, including speed calculation and problem-solving competitions. This may make arithmetic entertaining and engage for pupils and inspire healthy competition.

English: "Book Trailer" Lesson Plan

As part of this lesson plan, students will be asked to construct a book trailer to promote a book they have just finished reading. Students can use video or other multimedia forms to make a short promotional film for the book that focuses on the primary characters and topics presented in the text. The development of pupils' abilities in media literacy and their increased reading may be encouraged as a result.

Lesson Plan for Mathematics Using "Escape Rooms"

The objective of this lesson plan is for students to use their mathematical skills to get out of either a virtual or real-life escape room. Students may find mathematics more exciting and enjoyable, inspiring them to think creatively and improving their problem-solving ability.

Lesson Plan: Teaching Python (Computer Science)

Grade Level: 6th-8th

Subject: Introduction to Python Programming

Time Required: 10-12 sessions of 45 minutes each

Lesson Objectives:

Students will learn the basic concepts of Python programming

Students will learn how to write and execute basic Python code

Students will learn how to use Python to solve simple problems and create simple programs

Materials:

Computers with Python IDE installed (e.g., IDLE)

Python tutorial resources

Whiteboard or projector for displaying code examples and exercises

Lesson 1: Introduction to Python Programming

Introduction to Python

Explain how Python is a popular programming language for web development, data analysis, and artificial intelligence.

Demonstrate some examples of Python code and their output

Explain how to install and run Python IDE (e.g. IDLE)

Lesson 2: Basic Syntax and Data Types

Introduction to basic syntax

Explain the meaning of data types: strings, integers, and floats

Demonstrate how to create and print variables using Python code

Assign students to practice exercises

Lesson 3: Conditionals

Explain the meaning of conditional statements and their use in Python

Demonstrate how to use the if-else statement in Python

Assign students to practice exercises

Lesson 4: Loops

Explain the meaning of loops and their use in Python

Demonstrate how to use the for loop and while loop in Python

Assign students to practice exercises

Lesson 5: Functions

Explain the meaning of functions and their use in Python

Demonstrate how to define and call functions in Python

Assign students to practice exercises

Lesson 6: Lists

Explain the meaning of lists and their use in Python

Demonstrate how to create and manipulate lists in Python

Assign students to practice exercises

Lesson 7: Dictionaries

Explain the meaning of dictionaries and their use in Python

Demonstrate how to create and manipulate dictionaries in Python

Assign students to practice exercises

Lesson 8: Input and Output

Explain how to read input and display output in Python

Demonstrate how to use the input and print functions in Python

Assign students to practice exercises

Lesson 9: File Handling

Explain how to handle files in Python

Demonstrate how to read and write files in Python

Assign students to practice exercises

Lesson 10: Final Project

Assign students to create a simple Python program demonstrating the skills they learned in this course.

Give students time to work on their projects and provide guidance as needed.

Have students present their final projects to the class.

Assessment:

Students will be assessed on their participation, completion of practice exercises, and a final project.

LESSON PLAN: PHYSICS

Title: Introduction to Physics for Class 10 Students

Objective:

This lesson aims to introduce Class 10 students to the fundamental physics concepts and develop their interest in the subject.

Duration: 60 minutes

Materials:

Whiteboard and markers

Handouts with simple experiments and exercises

Videos and pictures to illustrate concepts

Lesson Plan:

Introduction (5 minutes)

Begin by introducing yourself and the topic of the lesson.

Explain to the students that physics is the study of the fundamental laws of nature and the behavior of matter and energy.

Give some examples of everyday phenomena that are explained by physics, such as why a ball bounces or how a light bulb works.

Fundamental Concepts of Physics (20 minutes)

Introduce some fundamental concepts of physics such as force, motion, energy, and waves.

Explain the basic laws of motion, including Newton's first, second, and third laws.

Demonstrate some simple experiments to illustrate these concepts, such as a pendulum or a rolling ball.

Understanding Energy (20 minutes)

Introduce the concept of energy and explain its different forms, including kinetic, potential, and thermal energy.

Discuss the principle of conservation of energy and explain how it applies to different situations.

Show some real-world examples of energy conservation, such as a roller coaster or a wind turbine.

Conclusion and Recap (15 minutes)

Summarize the key points of the lesson and highlight the importance of physics in understanding the world around us.

Provide some exercises or questions to reinforce the concepts learned in the lesson.

Encourage the students to continue exploring the subject of physics and ask questions if they have any.

Assessment:

Monitor student participation and engagement throughout the lesson.

Use formative assessment strategies, such as asking questions and providing feedback.

Assess student understanding through the exercises and questions provided in the handouts.

FOUR

Creativity Within Classrooms

By Teachers:

Creativity in the classroom is an essential component of effective teaching that helps to engage students and make learning more enjoyable and meaningful. Teachers can employ various creative strategies to create a stimulating learning environment that encourages curiosity and exploration and supports students' learning needs.

Teachers can foster creativity in the classroom by incorporating visual aids, such as posters, diagrams, and infographics, to convey information and help students grasp complex concepts. They can also use storytelling, games, and other interactive techniques to make learning fun and interactive.

Another strategy is encouraging student collaboration and teamwork by assigning group projects and providing peer feedback and discussion opportunities. This approach can help build social skills, boost confidence, and foster community within the classroom.

In addition, teachers can provide opportunities for self-expression by allowing students to pursue their interests and passions through creative writing, art projects, and other forms of self-directed learning. This can help to develop critical thinking skills, promote creativity, and cultivate a love of learning.

Incorporating creativity into the classroom can significantly impact student engagement and learning outcomes. By creating a stimulating and supportive learning environment, teachers can inspire students to take ownership of their learning, develop a lifelong love of learning, and achieve their full potential.

By Students:

Creativity in the classroom is not limited to teachers; students also have a crucial role in making learning happen. Encouraging students to think creatively and express themselves in unique ways can help to enhance their understanding of concepts and make education more engaging and enjoyable.

Students can bring creativity into the classroom by brainstorming ideas and collaborating with peers on projects and assignments. This can foster community and teamwork and help generate innovative solutions to complex problems.

Students can also use technology and other resources to create visual and multimedia presentations, such as videos, podcasts, and interactive simulations. These tools can help to bring learning to life, making it more interactive and engaging.

Another way students can showcase their creativity is through writing assignments, where they can explore their ideas and express their unique perspectives on various topics. This can help to develop critical thinking skills and promote original thought.

By fostering a culture of creativity in the classroom, students can take ownership of their learning and develop a passion for lifelong learning. They can also create a sense of self-confidence and independence, leading to more tremendous success in their academic and personal lives.

FIVE

TEACHING STRATEGIES

Here are some creative teaching tips and strategies that teachers can use to make the classroom enjoyable:

- *Use games and quizzes to engage students in learning.*
- *Use hands-on activities to help students learn through exploration and discovery.*
- *Use videos and interactive multimedia to enhance learning.*
-

Use storytelling to make lessons more engaging and memorable.

- *Use humor and jokes to keep students interested and motivated.*

- *Use creative visual aids, such as diagrams and infographics, to help students understand complex concepts.*

- *Use role-playing activities to help students develop empathy and understand different perspectives.*

- *Use music and sound effects to enhance the learning experience.*

- *Encourage creativity and self-expression through art projects and creative writing assignments.*

- *Use technology, such as interactive whiteboards and tablets, to enhance learning.*

- *Use analogies and metaphors to help students make connections between new concepts and things they already know.*

- *Use real-life examples to demonstrate how concepts apply to the world around us.*

- *Use hands-on manipulatives, such as blocks and counters, to help students visualize math concepts.*

- *Use open-ended questions to encourage critical thinking and problem-solving.*

- *Use visual organizers, such as mind maps and flowcharts, to help students organize their thoughts.*

- *Use multimedia resources, such as podcasts and videos, to provide additional learning opportunities.*

- *Encourage student participation through class discussions and debates.*

- *Provide opportunities for students to present their work to the class.*

- *Use peer feedback and self-assessment to help students develop their own learning goals.*

- *Provide frequent feedback to students to help them track their progress and make adjustments.*

- *Incorporate mindfulness and relaxation techniques into lessons to help students manage stress and anxiety.*

- *Use experiential learning, such as field trips and service learning, to provide real-world experiences.*

- *Use humor and fun rewards to motivate students and promote positive behavior.*

- *Use differentiated instruction to meet the diverse learning needs of students.*

- *Provide opportunities for student choice and autonomy, such as allowing them to choose their own reading materials.*

-

Use active listening techniques, such as summarizing and paraphrasing, to demonstrate empathy and understanding.

- *Use graphic organizers, such as Venn diagrams and concept maps, to help students make connections between ideas.*

- *Use small-group instruction to provide targeted support and feedback.*

- *Provide opportunities for students to teach their peers, which reinforces their own understanding of concepts.*

- *Use real-time feedback tools, such as online quizzes and surveys, to gauge student understanding and adjust instruction as needed.*

SIX

Optimising Teaching Within Schools

Here are some ways to optimize teaching within schools:

- *Provide ongoing professional development opportunities for teachers to continually improve their teaching skills and stay up-to-date with the latest teaching methodologies and technologies.*
-

Foster a culture of collaboration among teachers, encouraging them to share best practices and learn from one another.

•

Use data to inform instruction, including formative and summative assessments, to gauge student learning and adjust teaching accordingly.

•

Promote a student-centred approach to teaching, where students are actively engaged in their learning and teachers act as facilitators and guides.

•

Use technology to enhance teaching and learning, such as interactive whiteboards, online resources, and educational software.

•

Create a positive and supportive classroom environment where students feel safe and respected and are encouraged to take risks and learn from their mistakes.

•

Personalize learning by tailoring instruction to each student's individual needs and learning styles.

•

Incorporate social and emotional learning into the curriculum, helping students develop critical skills such as empathy, self-awareness, and self-management.

- *Emphasize the importance of critical thinking and problem-solving skills, encouraging students to ask questions, analyze information, and apply what they have learned.*

- *Encourage parental involvement and engagement, providing opportunities for parents to participate in their child's education and support their learning at home.*

SEVEN

UNDERSTANDING SCHOOL KIDS

The term "digital generation of school kids" refers to students who have grown up with technology and were introduced to digital devices and online platforms at a very early age. These students are considered the "digital generation" of school kids. Our current generation is very reliant on technology for a variety of reasons, including communication, entertainment, and education.

Despite the fact that technological advancement has resulted in several advantages for the field of education, it is essential to recognize that today's schoolchildren belong to the digital generation, which has a special set of issues that calls for special consideration and caution. The following are some of the ways in which they need to be cared for in this day and age of technological advancement:

Digital Health: Children in schools need to be taught about digital health, which includes being aware of the effects of spending too much time in front of a computer, being addicted to technology, and being bullied online. Kids need to learn how to regulate the amount of time they spend using digital devices, how to engage in responsible conduct when using the internet, and how to get assistance if they are affected negatively by the effects of technology in any way.

It is essential to strike a balance between the amount of time spent using technology and participating in other activities, such as getting regular exercise, playing outside, and interacting with other people. Inspire children to take part in pursuits that contribute to the maintenance of a healthy lifestyle and encourage direct interaction with family and friends.

Information Literacy With the plethora of information that can be found on the internet, it is crucial for school-aged children to develop their capacity for critical thinking and to become information literate. Kids need to be educated on how to judge the reliability of sources found online and how to distinguish between genuine and fabricated reports of events.

Children in schools need to be taught the significance of maintaining their privacy and how to keep their personal information secure when using the internet. It is important to educate children on how to create secure passwords, how to avoid exchanging personal information with unknown people, and how to spot phishing schemes.

Advice for Parents: When it comes to assisting school-aged children in navigating the digital world, parents and other adults in the child's life play an extremely important role. Parents need to be involved in their children's use of technology on a regular basis, establish firm limits for their use, and keep a close eye on how they behave online. In order to provide their children with the best possible assistance, parents should educate themselves on the most recent digital trends and challenges.

In conclusion, it is necessary to provide the digital generation of schoolchildren with careful attention and direction in order to maintain their health and success in today's technologically advanced world. We will be able to assist children in maturing into responsible and conscientious digital citizens if we place a high priority on their digital well-being, balance, information literacy, privacy, and the direction of their parents.

EIGHT

Digital Generation Kids

The term "digital generation of school kids" refers to students who have grown up with technology and were introduced to digital devices and online platforms at a very early age. These students are considered the "digital generation" of school kids. Our current generation relies on technology for various reasons, including communication, entertainment, and education. Although technological advancement has resulted in several advantages for the field of education, it is essential to recognize that today's schoolchildren belong to the digital generation, which has a particular set of issues that calls for special consideration and caution.

Parents, carers, and educators may struggle to keep up with the demands of children raised in the digital age. The following are some of the difficulties they could experience: Time Spent in Front of a Screen Children of the digital age spend a significant amount of time in front of digital gadgets, and it may be difficult to keep track of how much time they spend doing so. It is essential for parents and other adults who care for children to strike a balance between allowing children to use digital devices for educational and entertainment purposes and limiting the amount of time children spend in front of screens to reduce the risk of addiction and eye strain.

The digital age has given rise to a new kind of harassment known as cyberbullying, which puts children of the digital generation at an increased risk of being victimized by bullies online. Whenever a kid is subjected to any online harassment, their parents and teachers need to be aware of the warning signals associated with cyberbullying so that they can assist the child.

Overwhelming Amounts of Information Kids in today's digital age are confronted with an overwhelming quantity of information online, which may result in information overload. It is of the utmost importance to instruct children in screening and assessing the information they come across and to direct their attention to relevant and reputable sources.

Internet Privacy Young people of the digital age are especially susceptible to the threats associated with online privacy, including identity theft, hacking, and phishing schemes. Parents and other adults in charge of children's care must talk to them about protecting their privacy online and instruct them on how to do it.

Mental Health:

Due to this behaviour, children who spend significant time using digital gadgets may harm their mental health. Because of their online activities, they may suffer from anxiety, sadness, and feelings of alienation from other people. It is of the utmost importance to offer kids emotional support when required, as well as to urge them to maintain a good balance between online and offline activities.

In conclusion, managing children who are part of the digital generation may be difficult owing to the dangers related to the activities they engage in online. Awareness of these challenges and taking appropriate steps to ensure their digital well-being is essential. These steps include limiting the amount of time they spend in front of a screen, educating them on online privacy and information literacy, and monitoring their online activities to prevent cyberbullying and mental health issues.

Digital Well-being:

Children in schools need to be taught about digital well-being, which includes being aware of the consequences of spending too much time in front of a computer, being addicted to technology, and being bullied online. Kids need to learn how to regulate the amount of time they spend using digital devices, how to engage in responsible conduct when using the internet, and how to get assistance if they are affected negatively by the effects of technology in any way.

It is essential to balance the amount of time spent using technology and participating in other activities, such as regular exercise, playing outside, and interacting with other people. Inspire children to participate in pursuits that contribute to maintaining a healthy lifestyle and encourage direct interaction with family and friends.

Information Literacy

With the plethora of information on the internet, school-aged children must develop their critical thinking capacity and become information literate. Kids need to be educated on how to judge the reliability of online sources and distinguish between genuine and fabricated reports of events.

Children in schools need to be taught the significance of maintaining their privacy and keeping their personal information secure when using the internet. Educating children on creating secure passwords, avoiding exchanging personal information with unknown people, and spotting phishing schemes is essential.

Advice for Parents:

Parents and other adults play an extremely important role in the child's life when it comes to assisting school-aged children in navigating the digital world. Parents need to be involved in their children's use of technology regularly, establish firm limits, and keep a close eye on how they behave online. Parents should educate their children on the most recent digital trends and challenges to provide their children with the best possible assistance.

In conclusion, it is necessary to provide the digital generation of schoolchildren with careful attention and direction to maintain their health and success in today's technologically advanced world. We can assist children in maturing into responsible and conscientious digital citizens if we prioritise their digital well-being, balance, information literacy, privacy, and the direction of their parents.

NINE

Managing Google Generation

Handling digital generation kids may be a challenging endeavour for parents, carers, and educators. Keeping kids of the "Google generation" safe online might be overwhelming for parents, but it's crucial for their development. Here are some things parents can do to keep their kids safe while they're online:

Define Clear Boundaries Parents should establish clear boundaries around their children's use of electronic media, including the amount of time spent online and access to age-appropriate content. This will help youngsters develop good internet habits and safeguard their safety.

Keep an Eye on Their Digital Habits Parents should keep tabs on their kids' digital habits to prevent them from being victimized by cyberbullies or exposed to harmful information. Parents may utilize parental control applications and software to monitor their kids' activities online.

Educate Your Children About Digital Citizenship Parents should stress the necessity of teaching their children about digital citizenship and appropriate online conduct. They must highlight the significance of not sharing private information online, being considerate of others, and staying away from cyberbullying.

Promote Offline Activities: Youngsters should be encouraged to participate in offline activities such as reading books, practising sports, and spending time with friends and family. This will help kids create a good balance between their online and outside activities.

Parents should keep updated on the newest technological developments, concerns, and dangers. This will help parents lead their children efficiently and safeguard them from internet threats.

Communicate with Your Kids It is important to have an open conversation with your kids regarding their internet activity. Parents should speak to their children about the perils of the internet and how to be safe online. Also, parents should urge their children to report any inappropriate behaviour they encounter online.

In conclusion, parents need to be more involved in controlling the Google generation of children. Parents may safeguard their children's digital well-being and help them become responsible digital citizens by establishing clear rules, monitoring online activity, teaching digital citizenship, supporting offline activities, remaining educated, and speaking honestly with their kids.

Some obstacles they may encounter include the following:

Young people of the "digital age" rely heavily on electronic gadgets, and limiting their exposure to screens might be difficult. Parents and caregivers need to balance the benefits of children's usage of digital devices for learning and development and the risks of addiction and visual fatigue.

Cyberbullying is a rising problem in today's digital society, and children of the digital generation are especially vulnerable.

The use of digital gadgets may hurt the mental health of the next generation. Because of their online time, they may suffer from worry, despair, and loneliness. It is vital to encourage youngsters to maintain a good balance between their online and offline activities and to give emotional support when required.

In conclusion, dangers are linked with today's youth's internet activities that make managing this "digital generation" difficult. It's crucial to be conscious of these threats and to take necessary measures to guarantee their digital well-being, such as limiting screen time, teaching them about online privacy and information literacy, and keeping an eye on their online pursuits to forestall cyberbullying and mental health problems.

Digital Well-being: Children in schools need to be taught about digital well-being so that they may avoid falling victim to cyberbullying and other negative effects of technology. Kids must be taught to limit their screen time, to behave responsibly online, and to get assistance if they are having problems as a result of their use of technology.

Moderation: It's essential to strike a healthy balance between time spent inside and out, and between screen time and other activities like sports and socializing. Motivate them to take part in pursuits that will help them lead healthier lives and spend more time interacting socially.

Developing critical thinking and information literacy skills is crucial for today's students in light of the wealth of resources accessible online. They require training in spotting bogus news and determining the reliability of websites.

Children in schools need to be taught the value of privacy and the best practices for keeping their data secure when using the internet. Teach children to use long, complicated passwords, to never give out sensitive information, and to spot phishing attempts.

Parental guidance is essential in helping school-aged children navigate the online world safely and responsibly. Parents need to take an interest in their kids' digital activities, establish firm limits for it, and keep an eye on how their kids are behaving while they're online. As a means of better assisting their children, parents should also get informed on the most recent developments in the field of digital technology.

In conclusion, today's schoolchildren born into the digital age need special attention and direction to guarantee their health and success. We can aid in their development into conscientious and effective digital citizens by placing a premium on their health and safety online, as well as on their informational and digital literacy, their right to privacy, and the direction they get from their parents.

TEN

THE CHAT GPT CULTURE

An AI language model called Chat GPT (Generative Pre-trained Transformer) can mimic human conversational answers when given textual cues. Growing in popularity in recent years, particularly among young people. Students are increasingly bringing chat Group culture into classrooms for educational and recreational goals.

Chat GPT is a tool used in the classroom to help students develop paper topic ideas. Students may acquire a variety of perspectives on a subject by entering a question and seeing the resulting replies. Chat Talk also provides instantaneous translations and grammatical corrections, which may be helpful for students of any language.

Yet, questions concerning plagiarism and other forms of academic dishonesty are also raised by Chat GPT's usage in classrooms. The model's allure for students to plagiarize may have grave implications. Teachers and educators need to stress the value of original work and good citation procedures to students to address this problem.

Young people's exposure to Chat GPT culture outside formal education settings has increased, especially on online gaming and social networking sites. Users may utilize Chat GPT to develop clever comebacks, design their memes, and participate in lively debates with others in the chat room. Teens' emotional and social growth may benefit or suffer by using Chat GPT in online communication.

When used constructively, Chat Talk has the potential to improve one's ability to communicate and to open up new avenues for self-expression. Intercultural dialogue and the elimination of linguistic barriers are two additional ways in which it might help spread acceptance. Yet, neglecting in-person interactions in favor of Chat Conversations online might have negative consequences for a person's social development.

As a result, it's safe to say that Chat GPT culture is rapidly expanding at educational institutions and among young people. There are opportunities to learn a new language and express one's creative side, but there are also risks to consider in terms of academic honesty and making new friends. Taking advantage of Chat GPT while avoiding its pitfalls is a delicate balancing act.

ELEVEN

Teaching Through Mind Maps

Mind maps are a valuable tool to facilitate classroom learning as they help students visualize and organize information clearly and concisely. Here are some steps to effectively use mind maps for teaching in classrooms:

Introduce Mind Maps: Begin by explaining what mind maps are and how they can be used to help students organize their thoughts and ideas. Provide some examples of mind maps to help students understand the concept.

Choose a Topic: Select a topic you want to teach and create a mind map. Show students how to create a mind map by starting with the main topic in the centre and branching out to subtopics or related ideas.

Collaborative Mind Mapping: Encourage students to work in pairs or groups to create their mind maps for the topic. This will help students to collaborate and share their ideas.

Interactive Learning: Use a whiteboard or a projector to display the mind maps created by the students. Discuss the different ideas and connections that they have made. This will encourage interactive learning and allow a deeper understanding of the topic.

Assessment: Use mind maps as an assessment tool by asking students to create a mind map on a particular topic. This will help you evaluate their understanding of the topic and their ability to organize information clearly and concisely.

Benefits of Teaching through Mind Maps:

Visual Representation: Mind maps provide a visual representation of information, which helps students to retain information better and understand complex topics.

Easy to Remember: Mind maps are easy to remember as they provide a clear structure and a logical flow of information.

Creative Thinking: Mind maps encourage creative thinking and allow students to generate new ideas and connections.

Collaboration: Mind maps encourage collaboration and allow students to work together to create a comprehensive understanding of a topic.

In conclusion, mind maps are a powerful tool for classroom teaching and learning. They help students to visualize and organize information clearly and concisely and encourage collaborative learning and creative thinking.

TWELVE

Quality Circles In Schools

Quality circles are a vital tool that can be utilized in classrooms to improve the overall

quality of education and increase students' learning experience. They are also a great way for teachers to get student feedback. Individuals from different backgrounds join together to discuss issues and brainstorm potential solutions in the context of quality circles. Teachers and students in a classroom context may get together to establish quality circles to discuss challenges connected to the teaching and learning process and to brainstorm potential solutions to enhance the quality of the educational experience.

There are a variety of positive outcomes that may result from using quality circles in educational settings. To begin, it allows instructors and students to collaborate on analysing and resolving issues associated with teaching and learning. Students will feel more empowered to take an active part in their education as a direct result of our collaboration's creation of a more democratic and inclusive learning environment.

Second, quality circles give instructors a chance to get student input on the techniques they use to educate and the overall quality of the educational experience for the students. This feedback may assist instructors in determining areas in which they need improvement and in developing new teaching tactics to increase their students' learning.

Lastly, quality circles may enhance the overall quality of education by fostering continual improvement, which is another way to achieve quality improvement. The educational experience is continuously being worked on to be improved due to collaborative efforts by students, instructors, and administrators to recognize issues and locate viable solutions. Because of the emphasis placed on continual development, the quality of students' education is consistently improving.

Fourthly, quality circles have the potential to foster an environment inside schools that values innovation and creativity. Students are assisted in developing problem-solving and analytical abilities via the use of quality circles, which encourage students to think critically and creatively. These skills are essential for success in the contemporary world.

To summarize, deploying quality circles inside classrooms is a crucial instrument for boosting the learning experience for students and improving the overall quality of education. Quality circles create a learning atmosphere that is collaborative and democratic, supports continual development, promotes innovation and creativity, and provides instructors with the chance to get feedback on their teaching techniques. Students can play an active part in their education when quality circles are implemented in the classroom. This helps to create a more inclusive as well as effective learning environment.

THIRTEEN
KAIZEN IN SCHOOLS

Kaizen is a Japanese term that translates to "continuous improvement." It is also the name

of a concept that stresses the significance of continuously looking for methods to enhance one's processes, goods, and services. Since it offers a framework for schools to improve their operations and consistently provides high-quality education to students, Kaizen has become popular in education in recent years. Its popularity has contributed to the sector's overall growth.

Putting Kaizen into practice at educational institutions requires developing a culture of continuous improvement in which students, faculty, and staff are encouraged to look for places where they can make improvements and take action to bring about those changes. The emphasis is on making major shifts and creating little, step-by-step enhancements that will build up to significant gains over time.

The use of Kaizen in educational settings results in several positive outcomes. First, it makes it more likely that educational institutions will never settle for mediocrity and will constantly seek new methods to become even better. It is possible that an emphasis on continual improvement can increase academic standards, improve student achievements, and improve students' entire educational experiences.

Second, incorporating Kaizen into educational settings may assist in developing an atmosphere that values cooperation and teamwork. Schools can foster a feeling of ownership and responsibility among their students, staff, and parents by promoting participation in school development. This, in turn, may lead to increased engagement and buy-in from all parties involved.

Thirdly, introducing Kaizen into educational institutions may aid in eliminating waste and enhancing productivity. Schools can discover areas in which resources are being wasted and take actions to minimize inefficiencies if they continually evaluate their processes and procedures and look for such areas.

In conclusion, introducing Kaizen into educational institutions may be an effective means of fostering inventiveness and originality. Schools can generate novel ways of teaching and learning when they encourage staff and students to engage in critical thinking and generate new ideas. These novel approaches can potentially enhance student outcomes and better prepare students for the future.

In conclusion, putting Kaizen into practice in educational institutions is crucial for developing a culture of continuous improvement and ensuring that students get an education of the highest possible quality at these institutions. Schools can establish a learning environment that is continuously developing and improving if they promote a culture of cooperation, work to reduce waste, encourage innovation, and encourage all students, faculty, and staff to participate in the development process.

FOURTEEN

NEP- 2020 FOR QUALITY SCHOOLING

The National Education Policy (NEP) 2020 of India acknowledges the significance of technology in education. It emphasizes the need to incorporate technology into every country's educational system. It is impossible to deny the importance of technology in the educational process since it has become an inseparable component of our lives. The following are some of the most important reasons why technology plays a vital role in the educational system:

Increasing access to education Technology can democratize education by allowing students who cannot attend regular schools access to excellent education via alternative learning environments such as the internet. Thanks to technological advancements, students can now access educational materials at any time and from any location.

Adaptive learning strategies, personalized learning routes, and other forms of individualized instruction may all be made available to students via the use of technology, which can assist students' educational experiences to become more tailored to their individual needs.

Students may be engaged and motivated via technology, which can provide them with interactive and immersive learning experiences. This helps students feel like they are a part of the learning process. Introducing gaming elements into their educational background may make instruction more engaging and enjoyable for students.

Enhancing the effectiveness of teachers Technology may also assist in improving teachers' efficacy by equipping them with the tools necessary to offer effective education and track their students' development.

Because technology has become an inseparable component of our everyday lives, students must be taught how to make good use of digital tools to better prepare them for the future. Students can gain the skills and competencies they need to be successful in the digital era when technology is included in the educational process.

The National Education Policy (NEP) 2020 acknowledges technology's significant role in education and emphasizes the need to incorporate technology into all facets of the educational system. The policy proposes using technology to increase teachers' efficiency, tailor students' educational experiences, and expand access to educational opportunities. In addition to this, it highlights the need for pupils to develop abilities in digital literacy and computational thinking.

In conclusion, the use of technology in the classroom has evolved to the point where it is now a vital component. Incorporating it into educational settings may result in enhanced learning results, expanded access to educational opportunities, and improved preparedness for the future. The National Education Policy Framework (NEP 2020) offers a blueprint for incorporating technology into education. It emphasizes the need to maximise the sector's transformative potential.

FIFTEEN

Safety Anchors in Schools

It is of the highest significance to take measures to protect the well-being of pupils when they are on school grounds. Anchors of safety are precautions that are taken inside schools to make sure that both kids and staff members will be safe in the case of an emergency. The following are some crucial anchors for safety found throughout schools:

Plans for Emergencies: Each institution of higher learning needs to have a comprehensive emergency plan that details all of the steps that need to be taken in the case of a crisis. The plan needs to be evaluated and updated consistently, and the methods must be taught to the staff and students.

Fire Safety Fire safety precautions should be in place inside schools, such as smoke detectors, fire extinguishers, and frequent fire drills. Both the teaching staff and the pupils need to get training on the protocols for fire safety and evacuation routes.

Security Measures: Schools should have security measures, such as security cameras, visitor check-in processes, and secured doors. In addition, students should sign in before entering the building. This may assist in preventing illegal individuals from entering the school grounds.

In the event of a medical emergency, schools should have a person on staff who is certified in both basic first aid and cardiopulmonary resuscitation (CPR), and they should have medical emergency kits readily accessible. Also, the institution must have a strategy for how to react during a medical emergency.

Crises Caused by the Weather Every school should have a plan for how to react to a severe weather emergency, such as a tornado or a severe storm. This may involve having designated spaces throughout the school that serve as shelters and conducting frequent weather exercises.

Support for Mental Health Schools should provide kids access to mental health specialists, school counsellors, and crisis hotlines to better assist their mental health needs.

Safety in Transportation: Schools need to develop and implement policies and procedures to protect their children when they are being transported to and from school. This may involve requiring students to wear seatbelts, providing training for bus drivers, and doing routine safety inspections on school buses.

In conclusion, safety anchors in schools are essential measures that have been put into place to safeguard the safety of kids and staff members in the case of an emergency. It is very necessary for schools to have thorough emergency plans and safety procedures in place in order to guarantee the health and safety of all of the people who are a part of the school community.

About The Author

Dheeraj Mehrotra, MS, MPhil, PhD (Education Management) HC., a white and a yellow belt in SIX SIGMA, a Certified NLP Business Diploma holder, is an Educational Innovator, Author, with expertise in Six Sigma In Education, Academic Audits, Neuro Linguistic Programming (NLP), Total Quality Management In Education, an Experiential Educator, a CBSE Resource towards School Assessment (SQAA), CCE, JIT, Five S, and

KAIZEN. He has authored over 100 books on topics which include Computer Science, AI, Digital Body Language, NLP, Quality Circles, School Management, Classroom Effectiveness and Safety and security in schools.

A former Principal at De Indian Public School, New Delhi, (INDIA), NPS International School, Guwahati, and Education Officer at GEMS, Gurgaon, with an ample teaching experience of over Two Decades, he is a certified Trainer for Quality Circles/ TQM in Education and QCI Standards for School Accreditation/ School Audits and Management. He has also been honoured with the President of India's National Teacher Award in the year 2006 and the Best Science Teacher State Award (By the Ministry of Science and Technology, State of UP), Innovation in Education for his inception of Six Sigma In Education by Education Watch, New Delhi. Presently engaged as a Principal at Kunwar's Global School, Lucknow, India. Can be reached at www.authordheerajmehrotra.com

Books By The Same Author

OPTIMAL
CHILD
DEVELOPMENT
100 Tips For Parents
DR DHEERAJ
MEHROTRA
Now @Amazon

99 Ways
To Enrich
Struggling
Brains
Dr Dheeraj Mehrotra
Now @Amazon

Enter Caption

9 798890 025371

Printed by Libri Plureos GmbH in Hamburg, Germany